Down Syndrome

Angela Royston

Heinemann Library
Chicago, Illinois

Picture Research: Maria Joannou and Kay Altwegg
Originated by Dot Gradations Ltd
Printed and bound in China by South China Printing Company

09 08 07 06 05
10 9 8 7 6 5 4 3 2 1

Library of Congress Cataloging-in-Publication Data
Royston, Angela.
  Down Syndrome / Angela Royston.
    p. cm. -- (What's it like?)
  Includes index.
  ISBN 1-4034-5851-0 (library binding-hardcover)
  1. Down syndrome--Juvenile literature. 2. Mental retardation--Juvenile literature. I. Title. II. Series.
  RJ506.D68R69 2005
  362.196'858842--dc22
                              2004025852

J618.928588842
Roy

Acknowledgments
The author and publisher are grateful to the following for permission to reproduce copyright material:

Alamy p.10 (Laura Dwight); Bubbles Picture Library p.17 (Angela Hampton); Corbis pp.21 (Ricki Rosen), 26 (Stephanie Maze); John Birdsall Social Issues Library pp.20, 25; Mencap pp. 22 (Martin Sookias), 27 (Martin Sookias); Reuters p.11; Rex Features p.29 (Phanie Agency); Science Photo Library pp. 4 (Lauren Shear), 5 (Lauren Shear), 6 (Lauren Shear), 7 (Lauren Shear), 12 (Hattie Young), 14 (Lauren Shear), 16 (Hattie Young), 19 (Lauren Shear); Shout pp.13 (John Callan), 18 (John Callan), 23 (John Callan), 28 (John Callan); The Down's Syndrome Association (Lauren Shear) pp.8, 9, 15, 24.

Cover photograph of a boy with Down syndrome playing with friends at a mainstream school reproduced with permission of Science Photo Library/Lauren Shear.

We would like to thank Marie Benton for her assistance in the preparation of this book.

Every effort has been made to contact copyright holders of any material reproduced in this book. Any omissions will be rectified in subsequent printings if notice is given to the publishers.

The paper used to print this book comes from sustainable resources.

Words appearing in the text in bold, **like this**, are explained in the Glossary.

Contents

What Is Down Syndrome?

Down syndrome is a **condition** that some people are born with. People with Down syndrome are **affected** in different ways.

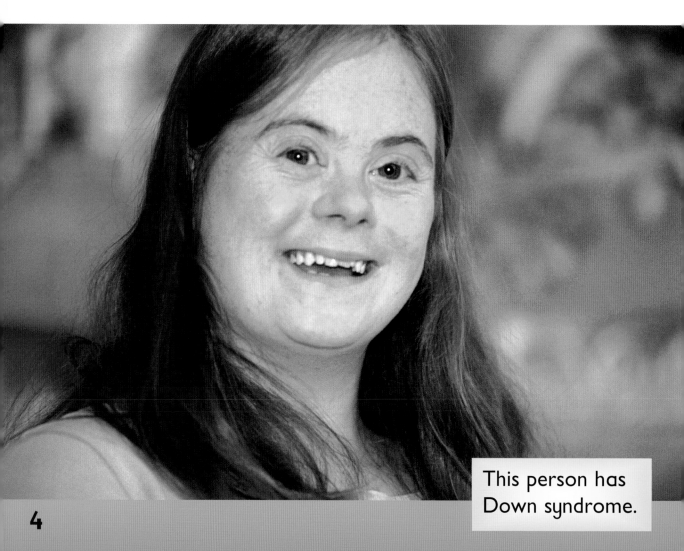

This person has Down syndrome.

Down syndrome is not an illness. You cannot catch Down syndrome from someone who has it.

Who Has Down Syndrome?

Doctors carry out special tests to tell if a baby or child has Down syndrome or not. This baby has Down syndrome.

These children are brother and sister.

In some families, one child may have Down syndrome but the other children do not.

7

Like Everyone Else

In most ways people with Down syndrome are just like everyone else. Sometimes they need a little more help than people who do not have Down syndrome.

People with Down syndrome may feel
happy, sad, or left out. Children with
the **condition** play with other children
and make good friends with them.

Learning

Children with Down syndrome do not learn as quickly as most other children. They usually learn to walk and talk later than most children do.

This young boy is enjoying walking on his own.

Doing something is the best way to learn about it.

People with Down syndrome **understand** more easily when they can see something. They find it harder to learn by just **listening**.

11

Moving

Babies born with Down syndrome may be slow to begin moving their **muscles**. Some babies are given special **exercises** that make them kick their legs.

Special exercises strengthen the baby's muscles.

As they grow older and stronger,
children with Down syndrome can
do the same things as other children.

This girl is good
at jumping on
a **trampoline**.

Speaking

Young children with Down syndrome often find it hard to remember words. They sometimes use hand signals as well as words to help make themselves clear when speaking to other people.

This boy is using his hands to describe what something looks like.

Children with Down syndrome usually **understand** much more than they can say. They sometimes get **frustrated** because they cannot always think of the words they want to use.

Reading and Writing

Most children with Down syndrome learn to read like other children, but it may take them a year or two longer.

Children with Down syndrome may take longer to learn to write and count. They may need lots of help while learning to write and count.

This girl with Down syndrome is learning to read with the rest of the class.

Extra Help

Some children with Down syndrome go to special schools. Here they learn with other children who need extra help to learn.

Many children with Down syndrome go to ordinary schools. A **classroom assistant** may sometimes help them with their work.

Seeing and Hearing

Many people need glasses to help them see properly. People with Down syndrome are more likely to need glasses. Not all people with Down syndrome need them.

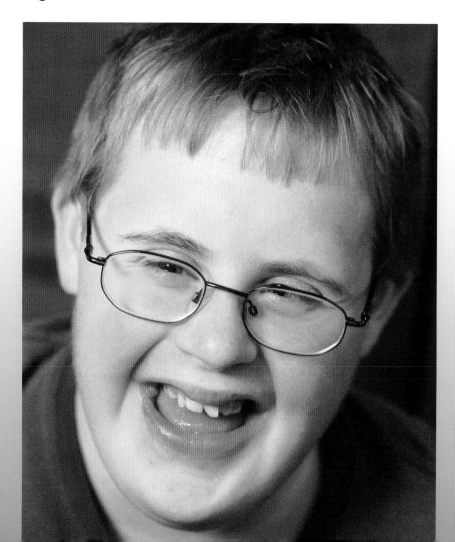

These children find it difficult to hear.

People with Down syndrome are more likely to have problems hearing than children born without the **condition**. Many of these problems can be corrected using **eardrops** or **hearing aids**.

Remembering Things

Many people with Down syndrome find it hard to remember things they have been told. It is much easier to remember something if it is written down.

People with Down syndrome often write
things down to help them remember –
just like people who write a shopping
list to remind them what to buy.

Having Fun

People with Down syndrome enjoy the same things as everyone else. For example, they enjoy eating out and going to the cinema.

A person with Down syndrome may enjoy the same games and sports as everyone else. They may also enjoy playing a musical instrument.

Living Without Help

When they grow up, people with Down syndrome may choose to live in their own home. They may cook and look after themselves. Some marry and have children.

This man has Down syndrome. He is using the internet to look after his bank account.

Some people with Down syndrome like to live where there are people to help them. Others live with their parents or family.

Working

People with Down syndrome do many different jobs. Some might be **photographers**, while others might work in offices or shops.

This person is working in a restaurant.

28

This person is making houses for birds.

Some people with Down syndrome work for **organizations** that provide jobs and extra help for people who need it. For example, this person is working in a craft shop.

Find out more

Apel Gordon, Melanie. *Let's Talk About Down Syndrome.* New York, NY: Powerkids Press, 1999

Bryan, Jenny. *Living With Down Syndrome.* Chicago, IL: Raintree, 1999.

Glatzer, Jenna. *Taking Down Syndrome to School.* Plainview, NY: JayJo, 2002.

Routh, Kristina. *Just the Facts: Down Syndrome.* Chicago, IL: Heinemann Library, 2004.
An older reader can help you with this book.

Glossary

affected changed in some way

classroom assistant person who helps a teacher or some of the children in the classroom

condition something that affects the way some parts of your body work

eardrops medicine that is dropped into your ear to help you hear more clearly

exercises particular ways of moving parts of your body to make your muscles, bones or joints stronger

frustrated feeling angry because you are unable to do what you want to

hearing aid machine that can help people hear more clearly

listen pay attention to something that you can hear

muscles one of the parts of the body that gives it the power to move

organization group of people who work together for a purpose

photographer someone who takes photographs

trampoline bouncy frame that lets you jump very high

understand know what something means

Index